LONDON MIDLAND STEAM doubleheaded

LONDON MIDLAND STEAM DOUBLEHEADED

W. A. Blake

D. BRADFORD BARTON LIMITED

Frontispiece: a pair of 'Jubilees' made as handsome a doubleheading combination as any of the ex-LMSR locomotive types, as witness No.45721 *Impregnable* and No.45567 *South Australia* heading up the 1 in 75 of Wilmcote bank in Warwickshire with sixteen coaches of empty stock from an excursion that had earlier worked down to Stratford-on-Avon from Glasgow. [T. E. Williams]

© Copyright D. Bradford Barton Ltd ISBN 085153 2489

Published by Enterprise Transport Books Ltd
3 Barnsway, Kings Langley, Hertfordshire WD4 9PW

Printed and bound in Great Britain by BPC Hazell Books Ltd

Scottish based Compound 4-4-0 No.40920 pilots Class 5 No.44995 north of Dumfries on 29 June 1957 with the 8.05 a.m. train from Stranraer to Dumfries.

Class 5 No.45394 and Royal Scot No.46106 *Gordon Highlander* with a down express approaching Northchurch Tunnel near Berkhamsted on 9 October 1948. The wartime era of notably heavy loads on the West Coast main line continued for several years after the end of hostilities and doubleheading was not uncommon.

[H. C. Casserley]

It was unusual to see the big Stanier Pacifics receiving assistance from a pilot but with this down express, No.46251 *City of Nottingham* has a 'Jubilee' (No.45630 *Swaziland*) coupled ahead; Berkhamsted, 6 November 1949.

[H. C. Casserley]

The 'Royal Scots' were beginning to show some signs of their two decades of exceedingly hard work and something like a million miles of running, by the date of Nationalisation. Of the class, 42 had been rebuilt by then and No.46137 *The Prince of Wales's Volunteers (South Lancashire)* – the leading locomotive of this pair – was in fact to be the last of the class to be dealt with in this way (in 1955). In the shafts – that is, the train engine – is No.6110 *Grenadier Guardsman;* Berkhamsted, 18 May 1948.　　[H. C. Casserley]

A freight at South Kenton on the up slow line with two Stanier 8Fs in charge, July 1958. No.48129 (leading) and No.48007 are both ex-LMSR engines, dating from 1935 and 1941 respectively, and both have the star symbol on the cab side denoting that they have balanced coupled wheels. [Derek Cross]

For main line duties as pilot there was nothing to beat a Stanier Class 5 – powerful enough almost to double the tractive effort on most expresses, and fast-running enough never to be over-run by the train engine. As the illustrations in these volumes show, the Black Five 'all-rounders' were perhaps the most frequently seen piloting class of all on main line work. In this scene at Kilburn High Road, three miles or so out of Euston, No.44940 is heading north with rebuilt 'Scot' No.46127 *The Old Contemptibles* on a Manchester express, June 1960. [Derek Cross]

The up 'Shamrock' passing Bletchley with Class 5 No.44866 piloting another of the same class. On the left is Eastern Region B12/3 No.61575 which has worked in on a Cambridge train. [S. Creer]

Rebuilt 'Patriot' No.45545 *Planet,* heading the up 'Ulster Express' near Welton on a day in June 1960, has the help of Class 5 No.45301 to handle the fourteen-coach load. Below; two 'Black Fives' near Welton on the same day, with a Euston-Manchester relief. No.44714 (leading) and No.45189 exhibit the differences there were between individual batches of Class Fives, of which many variations existed during their extended building period from 1934 to 1951. In both these scenes the M1 motorway is prominent, running close beside the main line for about three miles or so, to the west of Northampton. [Derek Cross]

A Euston-Birmingham express approaching Rugby headed by 'Jubilee' No.45738 *Samson* and 'Patriot' No.45507 *Royal Tank Corps*. [T. E. Williams]

A 'panned' photograph of No.45413 and rebuilt 'Scot' No.46142 *The York* & *Lancaster Regiment* at speed near Rugby on Whit Monday 26 May 1958 with an up Liverpool express. Extra loadings at Bank Holiday weekends always caused an increase in the number of trains needing a pilot. [M. Mensing]

Two Compound 4-4-0s, Nos.M935 (later 40935) and 41035, about to leave Birmingham (New Street) for Bristol on 4 May 1949. These were always rather light-footed engines, liable to slip on starting, and some adroit use of the regulators by each of the two drivers will be needed to get away clean here, particularly over the mass of pointwork which always tended to induce a slip.

[H. C. Casserley]

14

A Horwich Mogul and Stanier 'Jubilee' at New Street, 5 May 1958, waiting to leave with the 2 p.m. to Liverpool and Manchester. Leading is No.42814, with No.45567 *South Australia* as train engine. The Mogul will come off at Crewe where the train divides.

[M. Mensing]

A Newcastle-Cardiff train about to leave New Street station, headed by BR Standard Class 5 4-6-0 No.73065 and 'Jubilee' No.45663 *Jervis*. By the late 1950s the 'Jubilees' had become standard motive power on most expresses over this route. As in the earlier scene at this same location (page 14), the start away from the station will be tricky even for two 4-6-0s, for there are fairly severe adverse gradients up through the tunnels as far as Church Road Junction.

[M. Mensing]

Although divided from the usual Manchester section, with the latter run separately, the load of the 2 p.m. to Liverpool from Birmingham (New Street) on 18 May 1956 needs help on the first part of its run and 4P 2-6-4T No.42489 has been provided by Monument Lane shed (3E) to assist as far as Wolverhampton. The worst part of this section is the initial mile away from New Street, at 1 in 77 and partly in a tunnel where the rails are never dry, and the driver of the train engine, Patriot No.45538 *Giggleswick,* will be glad of the tank's assistance on this stretch.

[M. Mensing]

A morning Euston-Birmingham express approaching Berkswell in Warwickshire double-headed by Class 5 No.45301 and rebuilt 'Scot' No.46139 *The Welsh Regiment.* On the right are the lines to and from Kenilworth Junction and Warwick.   [T. E. Williams]

A pair of the once-numerous 0-6-0 Class 4Fs head out of Stratford (Old Town) on the Stratford-on-Avon & Midland Junction line, bound for Gloucester; 30 April 1957. Tender-first running was unpopular with footplate crews as coal dust always blew off the tender into the cab, despite periodic damping-down of the coal with the hose.

[T. E. Williams]

Two more views of freights near Stratford bound for Gloucester from off the Stratford-on-Avon & Midland Junction line, 8 May 1960. Above are Nos.44015 and 44175, again working chimney to chimney, and (below) Nos.43971 and 44219 passing Clifford Sidings.

[T. E. Williams]

A considerable tonnage of freight was moved from the East Midlands across to the South West over the Stratford-on-Avon & Midland Junction route and latterly 4Fs were standard motive power. They came from a wide-ranging number of sheds, from Bristol and Gloucester, to Bedford, Northampton and Leicester, etc. This pair (Nos.44317 and 44364) are from Bedford and Bletchley sheds respectively and are seen leaving Stratford on 25 February 1957.

[T. E. Williams]

Two views of a coal train from South Wales bound for Woodford (ex-G C) behind WD 2-8-0 No.9056? and Ivatt 2-6-0 No.43106, 8 May 1960. In the scene above it is approaching Stratford, with the newly laid connection to the ex-GWR Birmingham-Cheltenham main line in the foreground. Below, it is seen passing the former Old Town station.

[T. E. Williams

Doubleheading on Lickey; No.75009, of the BR Standard Class 4 4-6-0 series, leads 'Jubilee' No.45576 *Bombay* up the incline with a Swansea-Newcastle express, 12 August 1960. Helping at the rear with the twelve-coach load are two ex-GWR pannier tanks.

[Derek Cross]

Special excursion traffic was responsible for some of the doubleheading seen in steam days – as, indeed, is still the case today to a lesser extent with diesel traction. This scene at Streetby (on the Castle Bromwich-Walsall line) is of a fifteen-coach return excursion to Stockport in August 1957, run in connection with the Boy Scouts' Jamboree in nearby Sutton Park. Class 5 No.45403 is being helped by Ivatt Class 4 2-6-0 No.43022.

[M. Mensing]

The Somerset & Dorset route between Bath and the South Coast cut across some hilly sections of country and its route involved more severe gradients than one might suppose from a first glance at a map of the area. Doubleheading over the line was commonplace, particularly in summer when holiday traffic was at its busiest to and from resorts such as Bournemouth. In this scene, 2P 4-4-0 No.40698 is piloting 4F 0-6-0 No.44561 with a southbound train between Midford and Wellow. The 4-4-0 is working to Evercreech to be detached there and to help work a return north-bound train back to Bath.   [R. E. Toop]

In pre-Nationalisation days, when the LMSR operated the locomotive stud over the S. & D., double-heading was also common. This is 'The Pines Express' – as usual without any headboard – bound for Bournemouth on 23 July 1937 and seen leaving Templecombe behind 2P 4-4-0s Nos.631 and 635. These high-wheeled and fast running locomotives, with notably large diameter drivers, were somewhat unsuited to S. & D. operation but as 4-4-0s, with a leading bogie, ran safely and well on the sharp curves abounding.

[H. C. Casserley]

27

The other class that was standard on the S. & D. was the big Derby-built 2-8-0 with which this line will always be associated. Although nominally for freight use as originally designed, they were quite suitable for mixed traffic duties and in summer were regularly booked for passenger work. No.58800 is seen here approaching Radstock with an extra for Bournemouth, aided by 4F 0-6-0 No.44211.   [R. E. Toop]

Two unidentified Class 2 4-4-0s passing Midsomer Norton station with a train for Bath (Green Park) and Bristol; on the right 0-6-0T No.47557 is shunting the goods yard.

[R. E. Toop]

Back on the West coast main line, Class 5 No.44909 and rebuilt 'Scot' No.46103 *Royal Scots Fusilier* with 'The Mid-day Scot' near Rugeley, 1 July 1953. [Rev. A. C. Cawston]

A rebuilt 'Scot' and a 'Jubilee' teamed up to work the 11.05 a.m. Euston-Barrow and Carlisle on 14 September 1958. Leading is No.46166 *London Rifle Brigade,* with No.45582 *Central Provinces* behind. They are going well and not far off the 90 m.p.h. overall maximum imposed on the Western Division of London Midland Region at this date. Down trains on the section from Rugby northwards to Crewe were usually trying to make up the time almost invariably lost south of Rugby: in the up direction, most expresses were down on time at Rugby but could count on making this up on the racing stretch thence to Euston. [M. Mensing]

Rebuilt 'Patriot' No.45545 *Planet* and 'Scot' No.46170 *British Legion* near Rugeley with the up 'Welshman' on 30 June 1953. This express, serving the North Wales coast holiday resorts, was one of those on the ex-LMSR which seldom had a headboard due to the complicated diagrams of the engines working this express – as was the case with several other ex-LMSR named trains.   [Rev. A. C. Cawston]

A pair of 'Patriots' running light engine at Stafford; No.45506 *The Royal Pioneer Corps* and another named but unidentified member of the class. These 'Baby Scots' were fast runners and free-steaming, being more dependable than the 'Jubilees' in the latter respect, for the Stanier design was prone to give the footplate crew trouble if a tube or two was blocked.

[N. E. Preedy collection]

Class 5 No.45237 and Stanier 2-6-2T No.40087 with the 4 p.m. Leicester-Nuneaton local arriving at Wigston (Glen Parva) on 22 August 1959 – doubtless a doubleheading where the second engine has been coupled on to save an additional working 'light engine' through a busy section. [M. Mensing]

The ex-Midland main line saw a great deal of doubleheading in post-war years – as it had done much earlier – due to the restriction on the use of anything more powerful than 5XP 'Jubilees' into St. Pancras, (as 'Royal Scots' were not permitted to use the platform roads there because of clearance problems). With anything like a heavy load – with BR stock, a mere ten coaches – a pilot had to be provided to maintain booked times. Here Class 2P No.40485 and Class 5 No.45335 head a southbound express through Elstree on 25 May 1957. The overall speed limit on the Midland Division was also the lowest of any on BR at this period – 75 m.p.h. up to June 1956 and 85 m.p.h. thereafter.

[Brian Morrison]

4F No.44157 and Eastern Region B1 No.61219 paired up to work a train of empty stock through Apperley Bridge on the ex-Midland line from Leeds to Bradford: 29 July 1961. [P. Cookson]

An interesting doubleheader at Williamthorpe Colliery near Chesterfield, with ER Class J94 0-6-0ST No.68012 assisting 3F 0-6-0T No.47629 away from the sorting sidings towards the main line with loaded coal wagons, July 1967. [K. R. Pirt]

Ample power on the 1 in 100 climb away from Sheffield to Bradway Tunnel for this four-coach 'stopper' to Derby, March 1958; 2-6-0 No.46499 heads Class 4 4-6-0 No.73016. [K. R. Pirt]

The 4P compounds, like the 2P 4-4-0s, were popular for piloting duties and had the considerable advantage of coupled wheels of large enough diameter never to be in danger of being 'over-run' by a faster train engine. No.41165 is here assisting Class 5 away from Pontefract (Baghill) with a Newcastle-Birmingham express, 30 July 1958.

[P. Cookson]

The heavy Newcastle-Red Bank parcels was usually a doubleheaded turn in the 1960s; it is seen (above) passing Batley on the ex-LNWR line, hauled by Stanier Mogul No.42948 and 'Jubilee' No.45710 *Irresistible* on 10 April 1961 and (below) on 8 June 1960 passing Garforth Junction (NER) behind Class 5s Nos.45233 and 45156 *The Glasgow Yeomanry*.

[P. Cookson]

A Newcastle-Bristol train leaving Pontefract on the Swinton & Knottingley Joint line (owned by the Midland and N E) behind Class 2P No.40513, from Derby shed, and Class 5 No.45428; May 1958.   [P. Cookson]

The 9.30 a.m. from Manchester Victoria to Glasgow approaching Salford on 23 September 1961, doubleheaded by 4P 2-6-4T No.42653 and rebuilt 'Scot' No.46102 *Black Watch.*

[A. Tyson]

Class 5 No.44696 and 'Jubilee' No.45581 *Bihar and Orissa* leaving Ashton (Lancashire) with a local passenger train. The outlandish name of this 'Jubilee' came from two of the less well-known Indian Native States – sounds like a music-hall turn, as one Crewe driver put it when No.5581 was named in 1936 . . .

[N. E. Preedy collection]

A rare combination of locomotive classes, photographed in the marshalling yard at Rose Grove (Burnley), 24 April 1951. 8F No.48271 with a freight for Wigan has one of the yard shunters (ex-L & Y No.51336) to give her a pull up to the neck of the departure road at the top of these sidings. Worked by gravity, these were the principal sorting points for traffic into north Lancashire from West Yorkshire over Copy Pit. In fact a 'Lanky' saddle tank was unusual at Rose Grove, for 3F 'Jinty' tanks were the normal shunters used.

[H. C. Casserley]

'Black Fives' survived to the last in the North-West, along with the 8Fs: here, Nos.44874 and 45071, cleaned just for this occasion, are seen with a special departing from Burnley (Bank Top) in the mid-1960s.
[K. R. Pirt]

With steam off, 2P 4-4-0 No.40655 and 'Jubilee' No.45582 *Central Provinces* coast down Madeley bank towards Crewe with the 10.30 a.m. Euston-Liverpool, April 1958. Load limit for a 'Jubilee' on the Euston to Carnforth section was 14 bogies, or 13 to Special Limit timings. [M. Mensing]

In the mid and late 1950s, London Midland Region found itself chronically short of 6P and 7P locomotives for working the principal expresses – a state of affairs that was responsible for the initial decision, later deferred and cancelled, to rebuild most of the 'Patriots'. Train loads were heavy and the Stanier Pacifics and the 'Scots', however hardworking and reliable, were insufficient to cope. Thus, on occasion one might see a pair of Stanier Class 5s booked to work 'The Royal Scot', as in this scene on 8 May 1954, with Nos.44900 and 45317 heading the down train over the Manchester Ship Canal Bridge south of Warrington. Keeping the fire in good shape on such a long run with a narrower firebox than a Pacific asked a lot from the firemen but nevertheless Class 5s put up some worthy performances on occasions when deputising for the usual 'Duchess' Pacifics. Special Limit load for a Class 5 was 390 tons to Carnforth and 285 tons over Shap, enabling a pair to keep booked time with fifteen on.   [N. E. Preedy collection]

Another photograph at the same location showing yet another example of the costly amount of doubleheading necessary on the West Coast main line in the 1950s. 2P No.40673, from Preston shed, has been coupled on to rebuilt 'Scot' No.46155 *The Lancer* to work a Birmingham-Glasgow express. [N. E. Preedy collection]

Class 5 No.44910 and Jubilee No.45677 *Beatty* ease a long special from North Wales over the curves into Chester (General), beneath the ex-LNWR gantries at the down end of the station, on 5 July 1952. On the right is the former GWR shed and coal stage.   [N. E. Preedy collection]

BR Standard 2-6-4T No.80102 piloting Class 5 No.45275 into Bangor station with a special train destined for Butlin's Holiday Camp near Pwllheli. Class 5s put up some fast times on the North Wales coast line and speeds up to the 80s were not uncommon, although the chronic congestion on this section each summer meant that most of their running was more in the 'mixed traffic' range.

[E. N. Kneale]

A pair of local 2-6-4 tanks, with Derby-built No.42488 leading one of the later Fairburn series, entering the tunnel at Bangor with a well-laden Saturday Special for Butlin's camp at Pen-y-chain near Pwllheli, July 1961.   [E. N. Kneale]

Another pair of 2-6-4 tanks, Nos.42644 and 42574 from Trafford Park shed, run round their LCGB 'Conway Valley Tour' at Blaenau Ffestiniog on 24 September 1966. This long and scenic branch from Llandudno Junction was normally worked in post-war years by 2-6-2 tanks of Stanier build or by ex-LNWR coal tanks prior to that, but occasionally saw a Class 5 working over it.   [A. R. Butcher]

Class 5 No.44815 piloting 'Jubilee' No.4557 *South Africa* on a Workington-Euston train, a few yards north of Hest Bank water troughs near Carnforth; 27 April 1962.
[P. Cookson]

A Barrow-Euston express entering Carnforth on 18 September 1960 hauled by 2-6-4T No.42119 and Class 5 No.44897, approaching the junction with the West Coast main line before entering the station.
[A. Tyson]

The 2-6-4 tanks normally used for all-station locals along the ex-Furness main line helped out as pilots at busy times on over-loaded expresses. In this scene Fowler 2-6-4T No.42401 and Class 5 No.45141 are shortly due to depart from Barrow with a train for Manchester; 14 April 1962. [A. Tyson]

Class 5 No.45351 and one of its BR Standard derivatives, No.73132, wait at Grange-over-Sands with the 1.35 p.m. Barrow-Euston express, 31 August 1958. With a long train and a short platform, they are waiting to draw forward and stop again for the rearmost coaches.   [A. H. Bryant]

A pair of 'Jubilees' in good trim made a formidable fast-running combination. No.45674 *Duncan*, working back to Carnforth, pilots No.45631 *Tanganyika* with a Workington-Euston express in February 1962. They are entering Arnside station, having just crossed the long viaduct over the tidal Kent estuary.

[A. Tyson]

After a pause at Oxenholme to allow 2-6-4T No.42571 to couple on as pilot, this northbound express gets away on 2 September 1961 on the first uphill stretch of Grayrigg *en route* to Shap summit. This section of the West Coast main line route saw a great deal of doubleheading – a Class 5 for example being normally limited to taking eight or nine bogies at most unaided north of Carnforth. [A. Tyson]

Two Class 5s on Grayrigg bank doubleheading a Glasgow-Manchester express, 31 July 1959. No.45451 is leading the train of rather assorted coaching stock.

[N. E. Preedy collection]

After seven uphill miles from Oxenholme, 2-6-4T No.42594 and Jubilee No.45730 *Ocean* are still going well as they breast the 1 in 106 past the former site of Grayrigg station on 5 August 1960 with a Liverpool-Glasgow express. Note the tall ex-LNWR signal post refurbished with upper quadrant arms in LMSR days. Good sighting of signals on Grayrigg and Shap was more than usually vital for both up and down trains.

[Derek Cross]

Two Class 5s, with No.44778 leading, storm over Dillicar troughs with a northbound express, 5 August 1967. Taking water from troughs was a problem when running doubleheaded for only one locomotive could pick up at a time: here the train engine has overflowing tanks and the fireman on the pilot has his scoop going down to pick up what he can.

[John Goss]

Tebay shed had Fowler and Stanier 2-6-4 tanks as 'helpers' on Shap – classes which replaced ex-LNWR 4-4-2Ts in earlier days, as well as G2 0-8-0s on slower freights. This is No.42613 leading rebuilt 'Scot' No.46141 *The North Staffordshire Regiment* near Scout Green on 27 July 1957 with a down express.　　　　[R. H. Leslie]

Standard 4-6-0 No.75032 and Class 5 No.44948 attacking the foot of Shap with the 8.45 a.m. Morecambe-Glasgow, 15 July 1967. These Class 4s were used for a while as bankers and pilots here at the end of the steam era.　　　　[John Goss]

Fowler 2-6-4T No.42313 – piloting from Oxenholme as far as Penrith – helps Class 5 No.44914 on the climb of Shap in July 1957 with a northbound relief express. [R. H. Leslie]

With thirteen bogies behind the tender, No.44696 is well over the unassisted load limit for a Class 5 over Shap and has stopped at Oxenholme to take No.42613 as pilot to Penrith. The two locomotives are seen approaching the summit, heading a Southport-Glasgow train in July 1961. [Derek Cross]

Class 5 No.45044 and 'Jubilee' No.45556 *Nova Scotia* lay a smoke trail over the countryside as both firemen tend their fires on the climb south of Wreay towards Shap summit. The train is a Glasgow to Liverpool express on 3 April 1961.

[R. H. Leslie]

The Keswick Convention Specials brought some heavy trains from Penrith to the Lakeland resort and doubleheading of these was common – as it was also with other long distance expresses over the branch. In this scene in July 1967, a pair of the Ivatt Class 4 Moguls (Nos.43121 and 43120) are passing Penrith's No.1 signalbox heading onto the branch with the Special.

[Derek Cross]

The up 'Lakes Express' – one of the London Midland Region named expresses which carried no headboard - leaving Keswick on 6 July 1959, behind 2-6-4T No.42317 and Mogul No.42317. This is a change of duty for the Oxenholme-based Fowler tank which normally worked north and south either banking or piloting on the main line.

[R. H. Leslie]

The efficient little 'Mickey Mouse' Moguls became familiar on the Keswick branch working in pairs and Nos.46458 and 46426 were chosen to work a 'Lakes Special' run for enthusiasts in April 1966. After a rather unseasonable snowfall, the two locomotives are seen outside Penrith, specially cleaned and prepared for the duty. Other illustrations of this special working appear in the volume *London Midland Steam in the Northern Fells* by Derek Cross.

[Derek Cross]

The Workington and Keswick portion of the 'Lakes Express' behind Nos.46455 and 46491 on the 1 in 62 gradient from Threlkeld up to Troutbeck, 8 August 1959. At Penrith these two engines will come off and be replaced by a Stanier Pacific for the run south to Euston; they are from Workington shed and will work back there later in the day.

[R. H. Leslie]

Near-zero temperatures show up the exhausts of 2-6-4T No.42664 and rebuilt 'Scot' No.46102 *Black Watch* in December 1957 as they sweep round the long curve at Eden Valley Junction south of Penrith with a Glasgow-Manchester express. [R. H. Leslie]

The Class 4MT Moguls that were introduced shortly after the war gave good service notably in this part of the North-west and on the route over Stainmore, which gave connection from the North East via Tebay to the West Coast. This link carried considerable holiday traffic and excursions each summer from the industrial area around Tyneside to resorts such as Blackpool and Morecambe, as well as the Lakes. Here Nos.43073 and 43028 pull out of Kirkby Stephen and face the 1 in 60 climb to Stainmore summit with a Saturdays-only Blackpool-South Shields and Darlington train on 16 August 1958. [R. H. Leslie]

First of the class Fives, No.45000, with rebuilt 'Scot' No.46142 *The York & Lancaster Regiment* doubleheading a Glasgow-Manchester and Liverpool express past Wreay, south of Carlisle, on 17 September 1961. The two locomotives will part company at Preston where the train divides.

[R. H. Leslie]

Upperby shed at Carlisle had seven or eight of the Class 2 4-4-0s on its strength in post-war years which were frequently booked as pilots to help out with other hard-pressed motive power on the routes out of Carlisle. Here, No.40356 assists overloaded 'Britannia' No.70053 *Moray Firth* south up the long climb past Thrimby Grange with a Glasgow-Manchester express in May 1956.
[R. H. Leslie]

'Patriot' No.45541 *Duke of Sutherland* and 'Jubilee' No.45706 *Express* also near Thrimby Grange, south of Carlisle, with a heavy Glasgow-Liverpool express; 8 August 1954. This seven mile-long section at 1 in 125 is the worst part of the climb to Shap summit in the southbound direction.
[R. H. Leslie]

A final scene near Wreay to complete this trio of doubleheaders southbound out of Carlisle – No.45093 and rebuilt 'Scot' No.46105 *Cameron Highlander,* 31 March 1962. The train is a Glasgow-Birmingham, with additional through coaches for Plymouth.

[R. H. Leslie]

2P No.40673 and 'Britannia' No.70050 *Firth of Clyde* near Wreay on 14 October 1956 with a Glasgow-Manchester express. Below, Compound 4P No.41060 with another 'Britannia' (No.70054 *Dornoch Firth*) on the same working on 10 June of the same year. This was a rare class as a pilot here by this date.

[R. H. Leslie]

'Black Five' variant No.44756 and 'Scot' No.46133 *The Green Howards* doubleheading the up 'Thames-Clyde Express' on the climb between Smardale and Kirkby Stephen, 3 August 1957. This 'Scot' was one of the several allocated to Leeds (Holbeck) which were always well maintained and put up some record performances over the demanding Settle & Carlisle line.

[R. H. Leslie]

A few drivers thought the 2P pilots more of a hindrance than a help but were still booked to take one if their load was over the limit. At Carlisle (Citadel) No.46105 *Cameron Highlander* has No.40651 ahead of her on 20 August 1956 for the run south with 'The Thames-Clyde Express'.

[Rev. A. C. Cawston]

Heading home for Carlisle at the end of the day on p.w. duties near Ais Gill, two 4Fs (Nos.44326 and 43863) rattle over Armathwaite Viaduct on 10 June 1956 amid the beautiful scenery that characterizes the Settle & Carlisle line. [R. H. Leslie]